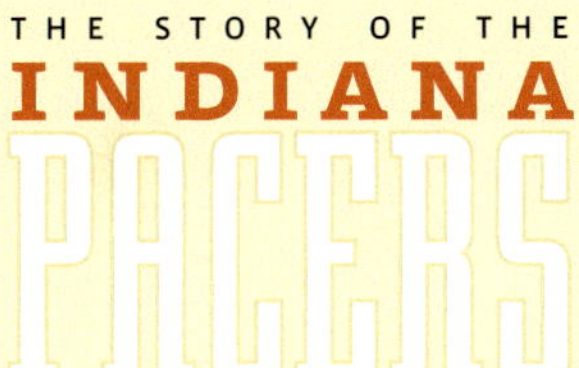

THE STORY OF THE INDIANA PACERS

CREATIVE EDUCATION

Published by Creative Education
123 South Broad Street
Mankato, Minnesota 56001
Creative Education is an imprint of The Creative Company.

DESIGN AND PRODUCTION BY **EVANSDAY DESIGN**

PHOTOGRAPHS BY AP Images, Getty Images (Brian Babineau / NBAE, Steve Babineau / NBAE, Brian Bahr / NBAE, Andrew D. Bernstein / NBAE, Nathaniel S. Butler / NBAE, Tim DeFrisco, Allen Einstein / NBAE, Elsa, Jonathan Ferrey, Bob Gomel / Time Life Pictures, Ron Haskins, Andy Hayt / NBAE, D. Lippert / NBAE, Mark Lyons, NBA Photos / NBAE, Noren Trotman / NBAE)

Printed in the United States of America

LIBRARY OF CONGRESS CATALOGING-IN-PUBLICATION DATA

Frisch, Aaron.
The story of the Indiana Pacers / by Aaron Frisch.
p. cm. — (The NBA—a history of hoops)
Includes index.
ISBN-13: 978-1-58341-409-5
1. Indiana Pacers (Basketball team)—History—Juvenile literature. I. Title. II. Series.

GV885.52.I53F75 2006
796.323'64'0977252—dc22 2005051410

First edition

9 8 7 6 5 4 3 2 1

COVER PHOTO: *Jermaine O'Neal*

THE STORY OF THE INDIANA PACERS

AARON FRISCH

CREATIVE EDUCATION

SPALDING
NBA
31

uarding Reggie Miller was no fun.

HE WOULD OFTEN GIVE HIS OPPONENT A QUICK BUMP TO THROW HIM OFF BALANCE, THEN DART ACROSS THE LANE, SQUEEZING HIS SKINNY FRAME THROUGH TRAFFIC OR LEADING THE DEFENDER INTO A TEETH-RATTLING PICK. EVEN IF THE GASPING DEFENDER MANAGED TO FIGHT HIS WAY THROUGH THE PICK AND LUNGE TOWARD MILLER AS THE INDIANA SHARPSHOOTER CAUGHT THE PASS AND SPUN TOWARD THE BASKET, IT WAS USUALLY TOO LATE. IN A POETIC AND IMPOSSIBLY QUICK MOTION, MILLER'S LONG ARMS WOULD LET THE BALL FLY. AND THE INDIANA CROWD WOULD ROAR.

INDIANA PACERS
Indianapolis Indiana

1

AN ABA DYNASTY

INDIANAPOLIS, INDIANA, IS LOCATED IN AMERICA'S heartland and is sometimes called the "Crossroads of America" because so many highways and railroads meet there. Moving vehicles also play a big role in the lives of many Indiana sports fans. Every Memorial Day weekend, the state's capital city hosts the Indianapolis 500, one of the world's most famous car races.

Indiaaa boasts a long and glorious basketball tradition at both the high school and collegiate level

Mel Daniels's dominance as a rebounder helped make him an ABA All-Star for seven consecutive seasons

But the pastime that Indiana residents—known as "Hoosiers"—hold most dear is the game of basketball. Basketball hoops can be seen in countless driveways and farmyards throughout the state. In 1967, Indiana was given a professional team in the American Basketball Association (ABA). Hoping to set the pace in pro basketball, the team's owners named the franchise the Indiana Pacers.

The Pacers were one of the original teams in the ABA, a league formed to compete with the older and larger National Basketball Association (NBA). After the Pacers went 38–40 in their first season behind such players as guard Freddie Lewis and high-scoring forward Roger Brown, the club made two great moves. The first was to hire Bob "Slick" Leonard as head coach. The second was to trade for center Mel Daniels.

Leonard was known as "Slick" because he always showed up for games wearing expensive suits—suits that quickly became rumpled as the fiery coach paced the sidelines and screamed directions at his players. Daniels, meanwhile, was one of the ABA's top big men. In his first season in a Pacers jersey, he scored 24 points a game, won the league's Most Valuable Player

ROGER BROWN'S RETURN

Pacers great Roger Brown started his basketball career as a high school star in New York City. But he was falsely charged with shaving points (playing poorly to help gamblers win money) and banned from both college basketball and the NBA. He worked in a car manufacturing plant for five years before the ABA's newly formed Pacers signed him in 1967. Brown's exile had little effect on his skills, and he became a scoring machine famous for his wickedly quick first step to the basket. "Sometimes it was so easy for him he would laugh at [defenders] and miss the layup because he was laughing," said Pacers center Mel Daniels. Brown became so popular in Indiana that he was elected to the Indianapolis City Council while still a player.

(MVP) award, and led the Pacers all the way to the 1969 ABA championship series. They lost to the Oakland Oaks, but a year later, they topped the Los Angeles Stars to bring home the 1970 ABA championship.

In 1971, the Pacers added George McGinnis to their lineup. Fans already knew the brawny young forward well, as he had been a dominant college player at Indiana University. In his rookie season, he averaged nearly 17 points and 10 boards per game. "McGinnis is so strong you'd swear he weighs 300 pounds," said Virginia Squires forward Willie Wise. "When he posts inside on you, there's nothing you can do. He's going to the basket."

McGinnis's muscle and guard Billy Keller's sharpshooting helped the Pacers roll to two more ABA championships in 1972 and 1973. Victories over the New York Nets in 1972 and the Kentucky Colonels in 1973 gave Indiana three titles in four years and a legacy as an ABA dynasty. But by 1975, the ABA was struggling. Attendance was dropping, and many of the league's top players—including McGinnis—jumped to the wealthier NBA. It seemed Indiana's glory days were numbered.

INDIANA PACERS

Known as "The Baby Bull" due to his great strength, George McGinnis was a frightening offensive force

NEW LEAGUE, NEW LOOK

2

IN 1976, FOUR OF THE ABA'S TOP TEAMS JOINED THE NBA. The Pacers were one of those teams, along with the Denver Nuggets, New York Nets, and San Antonio Spurs. The Nuggets and Spurs had talented young rosters that enjoyed immediate success in the NBA, but nearly all of the players that had led Indiana to three ABA titles were gone.

INDIANA PACERS

Billy Knight was the Pacers' first NBA star, netting 26 points per game in 1976–77 (second-best in the league)

Versatile forward Herb Williams spent eight years in Indiana without experiencing a winning season

The Pacers launched a rebuilding effort around two young players: smooth guard Don Buse and explosive forward Billy Knight. The 6-foot-4 Buse could score when his team needed it, but his primary duties were to direct the offense and play tight defense. In 1976–77, Buse led the NBA in both assists and steals. His nifty passes also helped Knight become one of the league's top scorers. "It's because of Buse that I'm having a great year," Knight told reporters. "He'll ask me if there's anything special I want to run. I tell him I'll do something, then I do it and the ball comes right to me."

Despite Buse and Knight's heroics, the Pacers struggled throughout the late 1970s. Aside from a winning 1980–81 season under new coach Jack McKinney, the early '80s were just as disappointing. The Pacers added talented forwards Herb Williams, Clark Kellogg, and Wayman Tisdale during those years, but they also said good-bye to Buse.

In 1986, Indiana took its first step in turning things around by selecting forward Chuck Person in the NBA Draft. Indiana fans—having never heard of Person—booed the selection. But the 6-foot-8 marksman promised to

THE PACERS SURVIVE

In 1976, the four ABA teams that joined the NBA all had to pay a $3.2 million entry fee, plus a certain amount of money to the ABA teams that folded. This put such financial strain on the Pacers that the franchise's very survival was in serious doubt. In early 1977, the team announced that unless 8,000 season tickets were sold for the 1977–78 season, the club would be sold to an owner who would most likely move it to a different city. On July 3, 1977, an Indianapolis television station hosted a telethon aimed at saving the Pacers. Ten minutes before the television program ended, the 8,000th season ticket was sold, ensuring that the Pacers would survive the transition into the NBA and remain Indiana's team.

win Pacers fans over. “I would have booed, too,” said Person. “But don't make snap judgments until you see me play. If you like basketball, you'll love Chuck Person.”

Nicknamed “The Rifleman” for his stunningly accurate three-point shooting, Person scorched the nets with almost 19 points per game in 1986–87 and was named NBA Rookie of the Year. With the help of guard Vern Fleming, Person and new head coach Jack Ramsay led the Pacers to a playoff appearance that year.

Indiana's draft luck continued in 1987 when the team picked up guard Reggie Miller. At the time of the draft, Miller was best known as the brother of Cheryl Miller, arguably the greatest female basketball player of all time. But Miller wasted no time in making a name for himself in Indiana. Like Person, he was an extraordinary long-range bomber, sometimes swishing shots from more than 30 feet away.

Still, the Pacers struggled as Miller and Person learned the ropes. In 1989–90, the team put together its first winning record in nine years. By then, Indiana had a balanced lineup that included forward Detlef Schrempf and 7-foot-4 Dutch center Rik Smits. These players made the Pacers a good team, but they were still no match for the NBA's most powerful clubs.

Although best-known for his outside shooting, fiery forward Chuck Person was a valuable rebounder, too

PACERS POWER

INDIANA MADE A NUMBER OF KEY CHANGES IN THE early 1990s in an effort to rise among the NBA's elite. Person and Schrempf departed and were replaced by such players as forwards Derrick McKey and Antonio Davis. In 1993, the team also hired Larry Brown—a coach with a great record of success at both the college and pro level—to direct the team on the court. "Larry comes in and wins immediately with what you've got," said Pacers president Donnie Walsh, "and to me, that's what a really good coach is."

Indiana was the fifth coaching stop for Larry Brown, who (by 2006) coached eight different ABA or NBA teams

Few players worked as hard as Dale Davis, a forward with a knack for pulling down offensive rebounds

Coach Brown lived up to his reputation in Indiana. In two of his first three seasons there, the Pacers won more than 50 games—something they hadn't done since their days in the ABA. But even with Reggie Miller's brilliant shooting, the Pacers seemed a little short on firepower when it came to the playoffs. In 1994 and 1995, they came up just shy of the NBA Finals, losing to the New York Knicks and Orlando Magic in the Eastern Conference Finals.

When Brown resigned as coach in 1997, the Pacers replaced him with Boston Celtics great and Indiana native Larry Bird. Although Bird was new to the coaching bench, he proved to be a natural. In his first two seasons at the helm, the Pacers returned to the Eastern Conference Finals. In 1998, the Pacers fell to the powerful Chicago Bulls, and in 1999, they lost to the rival New York Knicks.

Despite the losses, Indiana fans delighted in watching their team's smart and balanced style of play. Miller stretched defenses with his long-range shots, Smits added low-post scoring, forward Dale Davis dominated the

THE "KNICK-KILLER"

Reggie Miller played many exceptional games throughout his career, but he seemed to save his most heroic efforts for playoff games against the New York Knicks. In Game 5 of the 1994 Eastern Conference Finals, for example, Miller torched the Knicks with a 25-point fourth-quarter explosion. In Game 1 of a second-round playoff matchup a year later, New York was ahead by six points before Miller drained a three-pointer, made a steal, hit another three, and sank two free throws—all within 8.9 seconds—to give Indiana the victory. Both legendary performances came in New York as Knicks fans, including movie director Spike Lee, booed and taunted Miller. The hostile environment only seemed to make Indiana's "Knick-Killer" stronger, though. "He likes to be the bad guy," said Lee, "especially here at [Madison Square] Garden."

boards, and point guard Mark Jackson ranked among the best passers in the NBA. "We're not flashy," admitted Miller. "We play like our coach played—basic, simple, fundamental basketball. We move the ball, we dive on the floor, we play together.... We're a Larry Bird team."

In 2000, the Pacers at last reached the NBA Finals, where they faced the Los Angeles Lakers. Indiana gave Los Angeles and star center Shaquille O'Neal all they could handle, whipping the Lakers by 33 points in Game 5. In the end, though, the Lakers won the series in six games. After the loss, Bird stepped down as coach, Smits retired, Davis was traded, and Jackson left town as a free agent. It was time to rebuild again.

INDIANA'S BIRD

Before Larry Bird led the Boston Celtics to three NBA championships in the 1980s, he was the pride of Indiana. Bird grew up poor in a rural Indiana town called French Lick. In high school, the tall kid with the goofy smile set the Indiana state scoring record. Bird cemented his standing as an Indiana legend by playing college basketball for Indiana State University and leading the Sycamores to the 1979 college national championship game. After a 13-season career playing for the Celtics, Bird returned home to become the Pacers' head coach in 1997 and president of basketball operations in 2003. "I'm really happy to have Larry back where he belongs," said Pacers president Donnie Walsh, "and I think this is going to be the beginning of a new era in Pacers basketball."

INDIANA PACERS

Nicknamed "The Dunking Dutchman," Rik Smits spent his entire 12-year NBA career in a Pacers uniform

THE PACERS PRESS ON

4

THE PACERS REMAINED A STRONG TEAM EARLY IN the 21st century by surrounding the veteran Miller with talented young players such as Jermaine O'Neal and Ron Artest. Fans filled the new Conseco Fieldhouse to watch the 6-foot-11 O'Neal blossom into one of the NBA's most versatile big men and to cheer Artest's tenacious defense. In 2003–04, these players and point guard Jamaal Tinsley had Indiana rocking as they powered the Pacers to an NBA-best 61–21 record and the Eastern Conference Finals. They would go no farther, though, losing the series to the Detroit Pistons.

INDIANA PACERS

Unselfish and always-hustling guard Jamaal Tinsley led the new-look Pacers in both assists and steals

In 2006, the Pacers traded Ron Artest to Sacramento for sharpshooting forward Peja Stojakovich (pictured)

Indiana's 2004–05 season featured two big stories. The first involved an ugly brawl that broke out between Pacers players and Pistons fans during a game in Detroit and resulted in long suspensions for Artest, O'Neal, and other Pacers players. The second was the retirement of Reggie Miller after 18 NBA seasons. The star guard walked away as the league's 12th-leading scorer and its all-time leader in three-point shots. "His range was always something that caught players off guard," said Larry Bird, who knew Miller as both opponent and coach. "If you guarded him at the three-point line, that wasn't good enough. All he needed was a couple inches and he could shoot from any distance."

From their days as an ABA powerhouse to their current status as NBA contenders, the Pacers have long been the pride of Indiana. And sharpshooters such as Reggie Miller and big men such as Jermaine O'Neal have kept the Pacers among the league's most dangerous teams more often than not. Today's Pacers are intent on giving the Hoosier state's faithful their first NBA championship.

THE PACERS VOLCANO

In 2002, when the Pacers traded for Ron Artest, they knew they were getting a 6-foot-7 forward with the strength and quickness to tightly guard almost any player. They also knew they were getting a player with an explosive temper. In 2003–04, the Pacers got the good Artest, as he earned NBA Defensive Player of the Year honors. In 2004–05, they got the bad. In an early-season game in Detroit, a fan hit Artest with a drink, and the Pacers star charged into the stands, sparking a brawl between players and fans. After receiving an NBA-record one-year suspension and losing $5 million in salary, Artest expressed regret. "I just wish the situation hadn't turned out the way it turned out," he said. "I'm a big fan of the Nobel Peace Prize."

INDIANA

INDIANA

PACERS

Jermaine O'Neal, who jumped to the NBA straight from high school, was a multitalented All-Star

HOOPS

INDEX

TIME